Embodying Eden

Roots of a New Culture

Other books by
Lorian Press
(Starseed Publications)

Dorothy Maclean
Come Closer: Messages from the *God Within*
To Hear the Angels Sing
Seeds of Inspiration: Deva Flower Messages
Call of the Trees
Wisdoms

David Spangler
Manifestation: Creating the life you love
The Story Tree
Starshaman Home Mystery School[tm] Series

Lee Irwin
Alchemy of Soul

John Matthews
The Sidhe: Wisdom from the *Celtic Otherworld*
A Constant Search for Wisdom

RJ Stewart
Where Is Saint George?
(Starseed Publications)

Rue Anne Hass, M.A.
Opening the Cage of Pain with EFT
(Starseed Publications - English and Spanish)

Embodying Eden

Roots of a New Culture

*Nancy,
I hope you enjoy the book.
With blessings,
Jeremy*

Jeremy Berg

Embodying Eden

Roots of a New Culture

Copyright © 2008 Jeremy Berg

All rights reserved, including the right to reproduce this book, or portions thereof, in any form.

Edited by Freya Secrest

Published by Lorian Press
2204 E Grand Ave.
Everett, WA 98201

ISBN: 0-936878-18-5
978-0-936878-18-8

Berg/ Jeremy
Embodying Eden/Jeremy Berg

Printed in the United States of America

0 9 8 7 6 5 4 3 2 1

www.lorian.org

Acknowledgements

I would like to thank Deva Berg for all her artistic and loving support of my work with the Lorian Association and its publications. She is able to synthesize complex ideas and visions and draw out the meanings at the core, always adding something valuable to the mix. She also happens to be a wonderful daughter!

The interior illustrations and the cover art of this book, done by Deva, also appear as the some of the cards of the Manifestation card deck and Incarnation cards. Both decks were developed by David Spangler whom I also thank for his kindness and support of this book.

Thanks, too, to the love of my life, wife, best friend, advisor, and editor, Freya Secrest. You make the world a little more like Eden.

Let me also acknowledge Roger Harrison for his encouragement and for offering many helpful suggestions along the way.

Also appreciated are the many people comprising the Lorian community. You responded to my request for resources and continue to be willing to experiment, developing the rhizome for a new human being and culture to grow.

Dedication

To all our children and grandchildren and great grandchildren and all of their progeny. May they inherit a lush and healthy world from each of us.

The Purpose of **this** book?

This workbook is offered to outline and develop a basic core spiritual exercise called "Embodying Eden". It is designed to facilitate a connection and engagement with a richer life. This is a claim made by many but you might find this approach unique. It is my premise that the root problem of our time is not war, poverty, inequality, hate, or any of the usual seven deadly suspects. And it is not that we lack awareness of the spiritual dimensions of life, although this and all the aforementioned contribute to the issues we face. It certainly is not that the Earth is a fallen place or that the ego/personality is an obstruction to goodness. It is not that humanity is an evolutionary mistake and finally a plague on the planet.

The root problem, from my point of view, is that we are not fully connected and engaged with the fullness of our being and the richness of the physical and metaphysical dimensions of our world. We are disconnected from our wholeness and our world and give birth to fragmentation every moment with the consequences we see manifested on the planet around us, within ourselves, and in our societies.

How can this be changed? Well, this book is a start. Or rather, I should say that stepping into a state of loving connection with ourselves and our world and acting out of that engagement will give birth to a new way of generating the sacred on our beautiful planet. We can and will, through our loving perception and actions, truly embody Eden.

So ....

Are you someone who wants to make a positive difference at this critical time in human and earth history?

Are you someone who is trying to be what you want to see in the world?

Are you someone who wants to extend goodwill, health, and wholeness to your neighbors, friends and family?

Do you want to experience increased flow and vitality?

.... If so, this workbook is for you.

Humanity has reached a critical stage in its engagement with this earth. Global travel, communication and trade, high tech science, nuclear power and warfare, planet scaled pollution, computer intelligence, constant exposure to electromagnetic fields, information explosions, and bio-genetic engineering are all part of a long list of unique challenges and opportunities we are facing.

Birth of a new world requires us to claim our birthrights as new people!

We live at a time of great change and upheaval. This is said so frequently that it is easy to forget the special nature of our historical moment. Certainly many if not most peoples and civilizations faced catastrophes of varying types in the past. And, as the saying goes; the difference between an inconvenience and a catastrophe is whether or not I am experiencing it directly. Civilizations come and go. Mostly they have gone, but never have we faced the potential for human extinction caused by a war fought with weapons of planetary destruction. Never have we faced the fact that we are responsible for the mass elimination of other species whose extinction threatens our own viability on the planet. Never have we individually been so stressed, isolated and stretched to our coping limits.

On the other hand, never has the average individual experienced such possibilities for empowerment, for new vision, for self-understanding and wholeness, for unfolding new capacities, for giving service, and for making a difference. We live in a time when there is a growing and deepening appreciation of the potential blessing and power of each person and of the gifts inherent in incarnation itself.

It is this possibility within you, to make a difference centered within you, that this book celebrates. That is what this workbook is about, what it is designed to serve. It offers an approach based in love, action and wholeness. It is configured around you. You are the core of this workbook because I believe you can also be a center that makes a difference, from whom the possibilities and blessings of a new world can radiate. You *can* embody Eden and in the process draw out a new civilization from a time of chaos.

Personal Note:

I began this book in response to the Bioneers conference in 2007. It seemed to me amidst all the wonderful presentations of ecological science, social activism, indigenous culture, and other exciting offerings that some vital key was missing for a life sustaining civilization to emerge. This "missing something" has been my pursuit since returning from Viet Nam in 1969 with three purple hearts. It has inspired my experimentation with various spiritual teachings, prompted commune living, propelled a career in environmental architecture and education, and lives in me still.

This "missing something" is the seed of this book. I make no claim to be a shining embodiment of the possibilities contained herein but bear witness to a divine creative process at the core of myself in communion with the sacredness of the world. It is through this eternal "big bang" at the fountainhead of each of us that a new heaven and a new earth will emerge.

May you get a lot of bang for your buck!

Jeremy Berg 2008

"Someday after mastering winds, waves, tides and gravity, we shall harness the energies of love. And then, for the second time in the history of the world, man will discover fire."

Pierre Teilhard de Chardin

Table of Contents

Forward

Getting Started Pg. 1

    Warm Up Exercise: Pg. 7

Section I: Love Pg. 14

    1: What do I love about myself? Pg. 15

    Imaginal Exercise: Standing Upright Pg. 31

    2: Who do I love? Pg. 34

    Imaginal Exercise: Holding Loving Space Pg. 41

    3: What do I love about my Home? Pg. 44

    Imaginal Exercise: Loving Touch Pg. 59

    4: What do I love to do? Pg. 62

    Imaginal Exercise: Go with the Flow Pg. 75

Section II: Action Pg. 79

    1. What can I do to nurture myself? Pg. 80

    2. What can I do to strengthen those I love? Pg. 94

    3. What can I do to nurture the places I love? Pg. 102

    4. How can I nurture my natural flow? Pg. 112

Section III: Psychic Recycling Pg. 126

    Energy Exercise: Protection & Cleansing Pg. 135

Section IV: Embodying Eden Pg. 139

Section V: Where to from Here? Pg. 144

Forward:

Have you ever wondered what an anthropologist of the future, say the 24th century, might see if they could look through our eyes and out towards the 21st century. Driving down a congested freeway or flying into the polluted brown haze of Los Angeles or watching the nightly news; what questions would they be asking? Might they be trying to determine how we managed to pass through our dangerous whitewater rapids into their calm, bright blue waters? Might they be looking for clues as to how to confront their own challenges? No matter what the future holds we remain with the question of how we will avoid capsizing our vessel of civilization and navigate into a sustainable, just, compassionate, and free world.

Will we claim the future by imaging utopian societies? Will we design our way into the 22nd century with technically advanced technologies? Will solar power, wind and other sustainable energy sources be the foundation of our new economy and ecology? Can multinational business become benign forces for positive change? How about micro loans? Will we find ways to avoid continual smoldering war with fresh new negotiating and communication strategies? Do we just need an equitable distribution of wealth and resources? Are psychotherapeutic drugs or new psychological techniques our salvation? Will we find chemical or genetic ways to avoid crime, disease and starvation? Will nanotechnology save us? Are there new political systems still unborn? Will a new global village or religion spring forth from the internet?

Probably.

And it is the thesis of this book that none of these technical, social, religious, economic, scientific, business, psychological, philosophical, educational, or other strategies alone are sufficient to the task. They are all necessary perhaps, but not sufficient.

The reason for this statement is that none of the above address the pivotal issue, the Archimedean point of leverage. None of these approaches fundamentally change our functional and energetic relationship to the earth, to each other, and to our whole selves and hence will have unintended and possibly catastrophic consequences.

Albert Einstein said in 1946, *"the unleashed power of the atom has changed everything save our mode of thinking and we thus drift toward unparalleled catastrophe."*

It is not a just mode of thinking that needs evolutionary adaptation but also our hearts and ethics and spiritual connections to the earth. It is not just that *"We cannot solve our problems with the same thinking we used when we created them"* as noted by good ole Albert but that we must move beyond objective and abstracted thinking into a wholeness of being that shares and co-inhabits space with a world teeming with sentient life.

It is my contention that a civilization built on solar power or any other power may not be all that superior to what we already have if it develops without a deep appreciation of the spirituality of our own human being, the sanctity of others, and the sacredness of the world.

We need to become not just ecologists but ecologies. What does this mean?

We, especially in the west (which has become the dominant global consumer paradigm), have come to relate to our world as manipulators of matter and not as connected and engaged participants in the flow of life. Adaptation is required to listen deeply to nature, to actually hear the voices and wisdom of non human organisms. Evolutionary change is required to listen to the soul voice of humanity and the precious gifts it offers, *we offer*, to the planet. Transformation is required to appreciate a new emergent presence arising from our unique spiritual identity merged with our physical and supersensible selves.

A word about emergent phenomena from physicist Niels Bohr, *"Prediction is very difficult, especially about the future."* (I love this quote).

Regular table salt is an emergence phenomenon from two human poisons. This would be difficult to predict from just knowing the physical properties of sodium and chloride. Likewise water, the marriage of hydrogen and oxygen has odd properties (like being the only compound that expands when it freezes) which would be hard to extrapolate from their atomic structures. And, keep in mind that these atoms are mathematically and experimentally well described structures right down to their electrons, protons, neutrons, quarks and other strange, colorful, swirling particles.

Since we can't predict and certainly can't control what emerges from the combinations of even two "simple" atoms, how much more so is it true that we will not be able to predict or control the outcomes of our highly complex engagements with the physical, chemical, biological, emotional, mental, imaginal and spiritual aspects of our world? This was, after all, the message of the Jurassic park movies.

Generally we have not yet come to this realization as individuals or as a species. It turns out that we are extremely good tactical planners but inept strategists for long term species survival; our own and others. We cannot control what emerges from the primordial stew of our engagement with the world any more than we can control sunspots or hurricanes or the aurora borealis. We can, however, learn to improvise with heart and can develop the skills of playing incarnational jazz with Gaia. We can learn to hoist our sails and navigate in concert and harmony with the winds and tides and stellar flow.

The future will not be conceptualized or fully imagined or created on a computer screen. It must be lived as an emergent phenomenon.

Perhaps we need to evolve a new subtle sense and body. Perhaps we must become much more integrated with the organic flows of the planet; not just stewards or caretakers, conservationists, preservationists, or decision makers but engaged symbionts with the dance of biological and spiritual life on earth to truly *Embody Eden*.

We need a guiding principle for all of our interactions with the rest of life. We can no longer afford the hubris of thinking that we can predict the future when we introduce some new chemical or bio engineered product, or social system, or religion into the inner or outer environment.

We need a guiding principle that does not try to control outcomes but instead speaks to the underlying joy of our personal generativity working in collaboration with community.

Perhaps this guiding principle is love. Not some squishy universal steamy love fogging our future but rather a practical applied focused love that can power our respect, honoring, gratitude, appreciation, acceptance, and fostering; of each other, our whole selves, and the world. Love with staying power. Love with engaged will.

The understanding and practice of this love is what I understand the work of Lorian to be.

One final note. Niels Bohr, quoted earlier, also said, *"If you go flying back through time, and you see somebody else flying forward into the future, it's probably best to avoid eye contact."* Probably the reverse is true also so please keep that in mind if someone from the future wants to take a "peek through your eyes".

Getting Started

What more can be said about love?

So much has been said and demonstrated and written by so many geniuses of the spirit that it seems presumptuous to say anything more. Yet, this book is about love; how it connects us to our world and ourselves, how it engages us to become and create something new, how it transforms brothers and sisters and lovers out of strangers.

But love can also be intimidating. We have been shown so many examples of monumental love; love that transcends self, love that embraces all, love that knows no limits, love that heals the sick and raises the dead, that it can seem impossible to embody the possibilities.

So what is expected through this workbook and what is being asked of you when you are invited to love your world, yourself, others and what you do? Well, first let's be clear. You are not being challenged to love everything about the world, all aspects of your individual characteristics and every person you know. Will Rogers is reputed to have said that he never met a person he didn't like. Ok, but he probably never met some of the people you or I have and truthfully, we are not trying to become Will Rogers, some saint, or anyone else. And, quite frankly, the people I have met espousing a universal definition of love seemed a little distant for my taste and left me wondering about whether they actually cared about me!

Did you ever meet someone who claimed to love humanity but seemed to ignore the people in front of them? How about an environmentalist who, while installing solar panels, pollutes the world with a diatribe against multinational corporations? How about a spiritual teacher who taught love but was dominant and unkind to students. Have you ever encountered an aggressive anti-war activist?

The point is that we love not in the abstract, not in our ideals and programs, but in the down and dirty, everyday gritty engagements of life. We love specifically, and we need to appreciate the sheer unavoidable differences, limitations and boundaries of the other, whatever shape they take. If nothing else, environmental science has shown that even the least among us - plankton, cockroaches, wolves, and might I add, humanity - have vitals roles to play in the vast, interconnected web of life.

We need to start somewhere. And the place we have each been given is exactly where we are. We have a Gaia right in our backyard, everywhere we go we bring ourselves with us, and family, friends and neighbors are easy to encounter in the modern world.

Together we are trying to move from a state of relative disconnection from our natural ecology to a state of engagement with the sentient, organic life of the earth. We are trying to transform ourselves from feeling guilty and unworthy of health and joy and happiness to an appreciation of the gift we are to the world and to the Sacred. We are trying to begin building human relations based on love – and if not love then honoring – and if not honoring then appreciation of difference – and if not appreciation of difference then respect of life itself – and if not respect of life then harmlessness as a first step towards a world without war and nurturing of all life.

Doing these steps will move us toward embodying our whole selves and becoming our own, fresh, unique example of love in the world. We will become what we are, a gift of love and, with grace, experience both the oneness and the grand diversity of this beautiful earth realm of spirit.

This is a "How To" book. As such it is not really about psychology, metaphysics or theory. In a way it is like a scientific hypothesis waiting to be tested in the laboratory of your life. If it works, great, if not, then not so great for us all, but better to have tested and failed than to have not tested at all.

The hypothesis is this: we are all generative sources of spiritual life, light, love and presence for each other, for ourselves and for this beautiful life we call planet earth. We are all naturally, and without too much effort, stars waiting to be born.

Actually, to be precise, we are already stars generating a lot of varying "stuff" into our environment and collecting a lot of space debris along the way. Our star quality may not be all that apparent because of the soot in our gravitational field. We'll do something about that in the section on energy hygiene.

If we see ourselves as sources we step into a new relationship

> *There is an innate blessing process within us, which IS us, that organically crafts something that flows into the world around us, that creatively participates in, midwifes, and is called out by the ongoing birth of the world.*

with the world. No longer are we simply the effect of a mind-numbing cascade of causes or only a conduit for other spiritual forces; we become an artesian well from which a thirsty world can drink and flower.

That is how love is defined in this hypothesis, the ability to be a presence in the world capable of blessing through our own actions, inner processes and connections. This, of course, does not rule out working in collaborative partnership with others, be they alive or be they ……… somewhere else.

One might ask; from where does this generative power come? For me the answer is simple. It is the response given by mystics and sages down through history. At the core of our being is the Sacred itself (or herself, himself, themselves, or no self, or whatever other name you prefer). It is our essential nature to create new life since that is what sacred does. From this perception we are living in the first moment of creation! Unfortunately, restating this does not make me a sage, but, oh well, there's still time.

One more thing ~

It is, of course, ideal to try to care about whatever and whomever we meet, to see the sacredness of all things. The preferable mode of being is compassion for others and for ourselves. However there are dangers on this road to compassion. What happens if we encounter a person who just rubs us the wrong way? And, after really working with the issue - I mean really working the issue internally with deep discernment, meditation and prayer and externally with friends, therapists, mediators, lawyers, the whole nine yards - they still really rub us the wrong way. Do we condemn ourselves for being unloving? This can set up an internal downward spiral of self blame and failure. It is the classic inner journey of sham-an-guilt. (Yeah, I know, it's not that funny) Anyway, this can spread to a generalized feeling.

We would never expect a professional athlete to treat their failures in a similar way. What would it serve if Michael Jordan, after having missed a jump shot in the third quarter came down on himself in the after game press interview on national TV. "Yes, I did score 50 points and the game winning three pointer, but I am not a really a good basketball player because I missed that third quarter jump shot from 15 feet." Ridiculous you say? Well, we do this to ourselves all the time with love. We are sweet to our dog, love our families, give to starving children across the globe and even try to be nice to the telemarketers but kick ourselves hard when we can't get along with a co-worker. We say, "I'm not really a good, loving, kind person because if I was I could get over this issue." Live with it! Be like Mike; keep shooting the jump shot and more will go in.

Let's get to it!

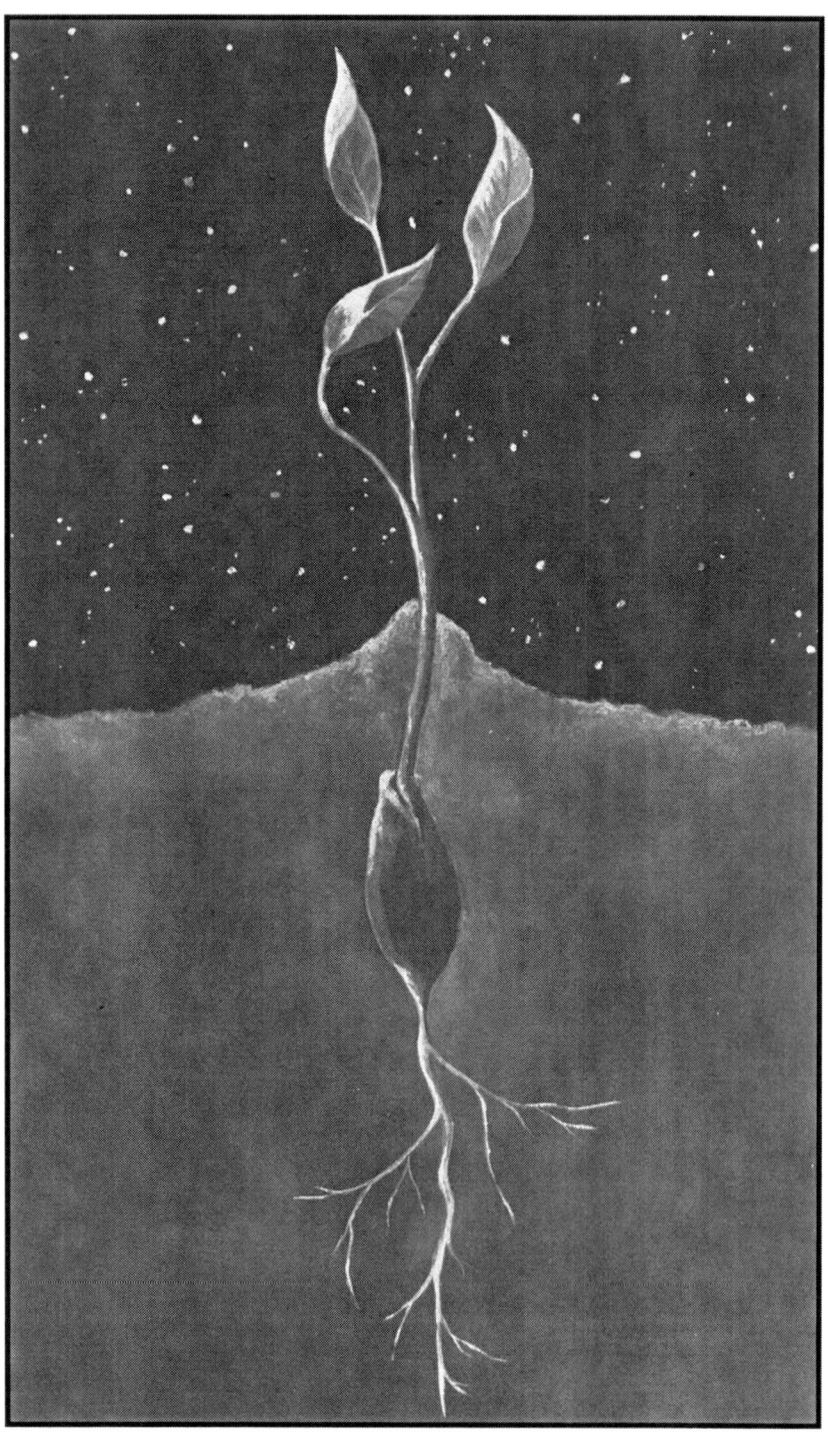

Warm Up Exercise

Stop and Smell the Forest

As you begin working with these questions you will note that there is no place where you are asked to list your negative traits, your challenges with other people, what you dislike about your surroundings, or your problems with your work. This may seem overly optimistic or unbalanced toward the positive. After all, life is full of challenges and we all know in our private moments that we are less that perfect. Why then only look at the bright side?

There are two answers to this question. The first is a practical, psychological one. We live in a sticky world and it is easy to take on the negative impressions of others and of the world and internalize them. It is healthy occasionally to step back and acknowledge the good and beautiful and true in ourselves and our surroundings. Evolutionary biologists tell us that there may be a competitive advantage to doing so.

However, this is not the main reason for this approach. The second and main reason is that this entire book is not intended as a growth technique. It does not offer spiritual development, whatever that is, toward some initiatory plateau. Nor does it seek to give you techniques to transmute negatives into positives. The intent is to try to offer something that allows you to experience and perhaps strengthen the healthy connections you already enjoy within yourself, with others, with your surroundings and with your activities. On whatever path you may be treading my suggestion is that you stop and smell the roses. There is a deep wisdom in this simple saying; it does not suggest stopping to smell the compost or manure. And I might alter this aphorism a bit and say – stop and smell the forest – it has a wonderful scent all of its own. The forest of us, the forest of our relationships, the forest of our overall surrounding and activities has a wonderful, earthy, organic aroma unique to and for each of us. It suggests that wherever we are going we will arrive there faster, healthier and with more surety if we pay attention to the actual sacred experience of being ourselves, walking on a path, with companions, in the forest.

Here is a short imaginal exercise to get us going in that direction.

Stop and Smell the **Forest**

Imagine that you are an acorn imbedded in the dark soil. You are quiet, warm, snuggled in, nurtured by the womb of your surroundings. You are at peace and one with the earth. Yet you are aware of being something unique. You imagine a bright light drawing you out to larger expressions. You feel the stirring of the spring rains and other lives wiggling in the land. You begin to push out, fueled by inchoate dreams and visions of unknown places. You curl out from yourself in an ancient ritual, too new to name. You break into the light of the Milky Way, into the inner realms of sunlight and breezes, of pungent smells, vibrations and chewing things. Your roots plunge deep and search wide for stable rock and water and food.

You synthesize the light, the water and the nutrients of the soil. You inhale your destiny in the chemistry of the woods. Sap flows, heartwood grows, fecund acorns fall. Fires roar, insects bore, branches break in heavy storms, birds and squirrels nest, leaves fall. You become strong and old and take your place in the forest primeval. In winter each twisted branch and gnarled root and charred section of your bark bears witness to your struggles, your perseverance and your fractal patterns of growth. Each summer celebrates your green, sensuous joy.

Many seasons come and go. You blow over in a strong wind and melt back into the dark soil. Your memories are full. You are quiet, warm, snuggled in, nurtured by the womb of your surroundings.

This is the regular cycle of a tree there for all to see. It can be viewed as a metaphor for our lives or of a spiritual journey back to Eden.

However, I would like to leave you with these questions, Koans if you will, which are the main point of the exercise.

When did you feel closest to the essence of being a tree?

When did you feel fully part of the ecology of the forest, the earth, and the cosmos?

During what cycle of activity were you acting most like a tree?

Eden is described as the place where we once communed with God.

When in our growth are we closest to sacredness and to **Embodying Eden***?*

.... Notes on the Exercise ....

.... Reflections on the Questions ....

....Notes on Group Discussions....

Section I: **Love**

In this section we begin a process of self reflection and discovery. This is not a hard thing to do and it certainly should not be stressful. What is being asked for is that you begin to remember your connections to the place you live, to honor yourself in a new way, and to appreciate those with whom you choose to be most intimate.

This section is divided into four questions:

1. *What do I love about myself?*

2. *Who do I love?*

3. *What do I love about my place?*

4. *What do I love to do?*

On the following pages provided please reflect on these questions taking a week or so with each of the four. You will note that there are a few starter questions in each area to get you going.
If these help, use them. **Otherwise, please feel free to use just some of them or add others**. Do what comes naturally in response to the overall question.
The idea here is to begin to align with your natural love and engagement with your place, yourselves, each other and your activities. Once we have done that we have begun to incarnate more fully into our lives. This provides a natural bridge to deeper work and more extensive service, but for now just enjoy swimming in the refreshing currents of your own love and joy in the world.

First Question:

What do I love about myself?

my qualities
my talents
my ethics
my history
my ancestry
my body
my spirit
my _____?

These are my **best** qualities

Name at least five. Stand and appreciate yourself. Find things like perseverance, humor, reverence, humility, patience, honesty, friendliness, or kindness. Are you happy-go-lucky, strong, faithful, exuberant, spiritual, irreverent, ethical? Everybody brings a unique mix of qualities all their own; just like trace minerals, they are vitally needed to support complex living systems like our bodies and the world. Find someone who really likes you and have them make a list about you.

.... Personal list ....

_____

_____

_____

_____

_____

_____

_____

_____

_____

_____

_____

_____

_____

•••• *Friend's list* ••••

•••• *Reflections* ••••

These are my talents

Everyone has talent, some special gifts or capacities that seems to have been given extra genetic and soul emphasis. Sometimes this can be hard to describe as it may not be obvious like musical or mathematical or athletic talent. Look hard, you will find many!

.... Talent list ....

_____
_____
_____
_____
_____
_____
_____
_____
_____
_____
_____
_____
_____
_____
_____
_____
_____
_____
_____

This is what I love about my personal history

What have you experienced in your life that gives it special positive meaning? What would you put on the plus side in your memoirs at this point in your life? What has contributed to shape the unique individual that you are today? Describe the silver linings of your challenges. When have you made lemonade out of lemons?

....Building Blocks....

_____

_____

_____

_____

_____

_____

_____

_____

_____

_____

_____

_____

Here is what I love about my
personal ancestry

Our ancestry is much more complex than we normally appreciate. Genetic testing shows humans to be 99.99% genetically identical, but, oh, that .01%! We come from a long line of Homo Sapiens at least 150,000 years in the making. Bipedal primates have been practicing standing upright for over 6 million years. We can trace our lineage back to the beginning of organic life some 3.5 BILLION years here on earth. Each cell in our body is a direct descendant of the first cell on earth. Who knows what preceded that. Closer to home, we each carry an indigenous heritage of the story of humanity. What is your story?

....Genetic Ancestry....

_____
_____
_____
_____
_____
_____
_____
_____
_____
_____
_____

.... *Spiritual Lineage* ....

What I love about
my body

Even if we don't like the current shape of our body (who does?) we can appreciate how it functions, how it retains its ancient wisdom, how is roots us to biological life and how it is our most intimate ally and connection to this beautiful earth.

....Body Appreciations....

What I love about
my Spirit

Body and spirit are closely linked, two rooms of the same house. What is it about your spirit that fills you with gratitude? Have you ever been surprised by some action that seemed to be "outside yourself" and yet you entered into it naturally in the moment? If you were a bird what kind would you be? Where would you soar?

..... Spirit Gratitude .....

_____
_____
_____
_____
_____
_____
_____
_____
_____
_____
_____
_____
_____
_____

I love my _____

(Name another aspect of yourself)

···· Notes ····

.... Reflections on Loving Myself ....

.... Reflections on Loving Myself ....

_____

_____

_____

_____

_____

_____

_____

_____

_____

_____

_____

_____

_____

    Many wise people, including Jesus, have noted that we should love our neighbors as ourselves. Perhaps this is part of the problem. By not actively loving ourselves and by not appreciating our own body/mind/heart/spirit we have trouble honoring others and blessing our world. Perhaps these reflective exercises have helped in that regard. I certainly hope so.

    This first question of the first section ends with an *Imaginal* exercise. This is a pattern we will follow for the entire book.

···· Notes on Group Discussions ····

First *Imaginal* Exercise
Standing **Upright**

Stand up! Feel the physical power of standing upright!

Now, please list for yourself several times when you felt you were standing strongly, gracefully and fully in yourself and/or in the world.

Perhaps it was a time you happily stood up for yourself or someone else. Maybe it was a time you had a cherished chance to stand for something you love deeply. Perhaps it was some event that put you in good standing after a job well done. It could be a situation that simply gave you a wonderful sense of safety and well being, a sense of being really alive in this breath-taking and breath-giving world.

What is being asked for here is a past experience that you can vividly recall in which you felt a strong sense of creative, loving, calm, joyful, clear and powerful identity.

Then pick one of the times and describe it. What did it feel like in your body, in your mind and emotions, in your heart and soul?

What are the qualities that you exhibit when you are expressing out of this clear and loving identity? This is the beginning of appreciating the vast power of the incarnating self.

.... List of My Standing Experiences ....

.... *Detailed Description* ....

Second Question

Who do I love?
&
What are their special qualities?

Who do I Love?

First make a list of the ten (or two or twenty) people with whom you are most intimate. Revel in the fact that you can be intimate, can love someone else and can care and nurture them. What do you feel when you think of them, when you hold them in your heart. What space develops in and around you while doing so?

..... List of Favorite People ....

_____
_____
_____
_____
_____
_____
_____
_____
_____
_____
_____
_____
_____
_____
_____

Here are the unique qualities of
each person I love

In this area simply name the person and write down what makes them special to you. Perhaps it is something indefinable but try to give it a name or try to give the "felt sense" of their presence a name. Listen to your body; what does it feel like to imagine this person in your heart?

.... *Person and Qualities* ....

_____
_____
_____
_____
_____
_____

.... *Person and Qualities* ....

_____
_____
_____
_____
_____
_____

....Person and Qualities....

_____
_____
_____
_____
_____
_____
_____

....Person and Qualities....

_____
_____
_____
_____
_____
_____
_____

....Person and Qualities....

_____
_____
_____
_____
_____
_____
_____

....Person and Qualities....

_____
_____
_____
_____
_____
_____

....Person and Qualities....

_____
_____
_____
_____
_____
_____

....Person and Qualities....

_____
_____
_____
_____
_____
_____

.... Notes on Group Discussions ....

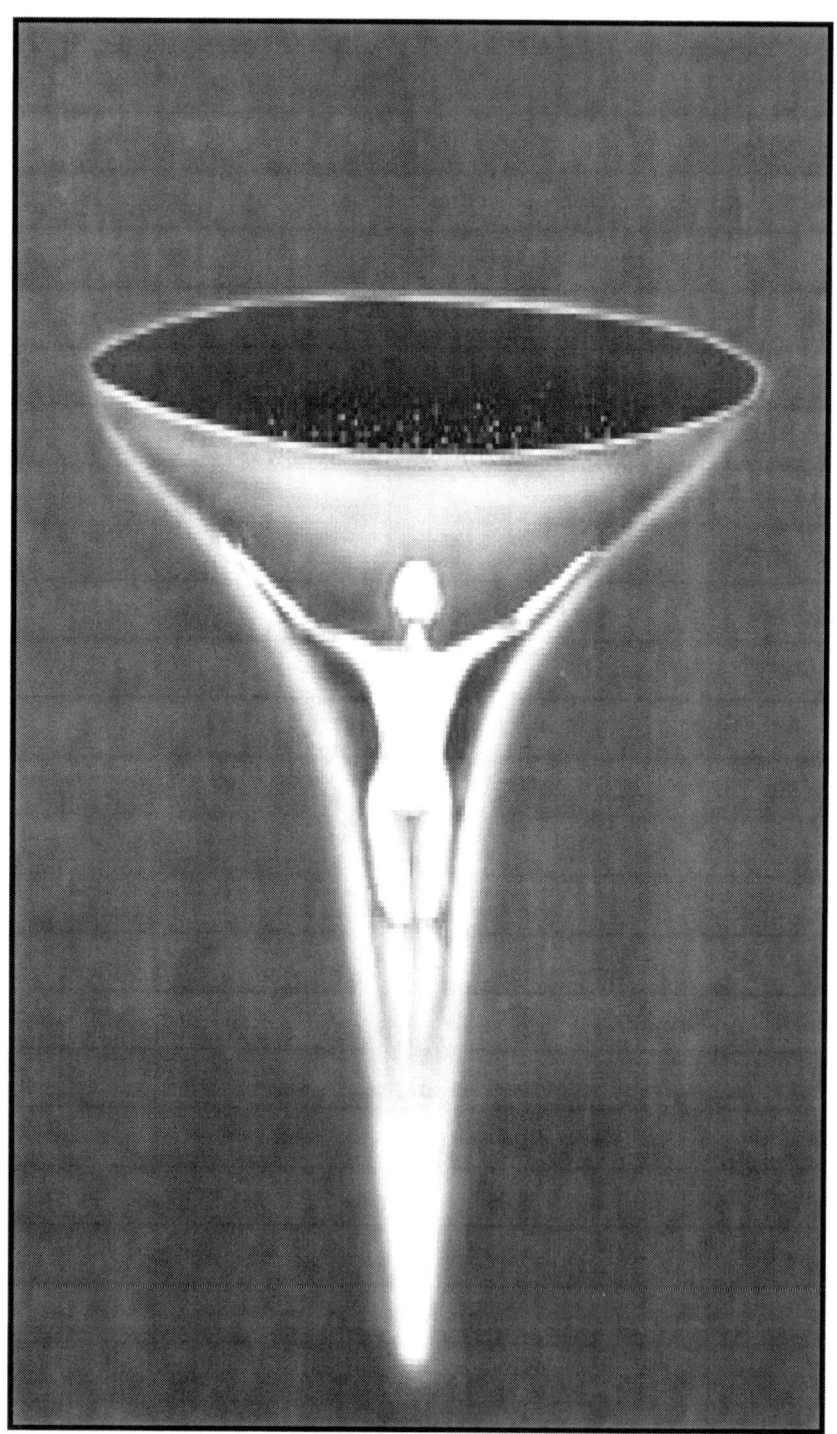

Second Imaginal Exercise
Holding loving Space

Hold someone or something you love! Let your pet sit on your lap for awhile! Hug a tree or a child!

On the following page please list for yourself several times in which you felt you were holding someone in a nurturing, loving space. Imagine holding a baby on your lap or a friend in need. Perhaps it was one of your children on stage for the first time and you held them (while holding your breath too) in a deep wish for their success in the world. Perhaps you held someone while they died.

*What is being asked for here is a past experience that you can vividly recall in which you felt a strong sense of creative, loving, calm, joyful, clear and powerful **holding**.*

Then pick one of the times and describe it. What did it feel like in your body, in your mind and emotions, in your heart and soul?

What are the qualities that you exhibit when you are holding in this manner?

.... List of My Holding Experiences ....

.... Detailed Description ....

Third Question

What do I love about my:

home
neighborhood
town or city
bioregion
world
historical time
special space or place
&
my overall physical universe

What about my home do I love?

Our homes are special to us. We create them out of our interaction with the architecture, the interior spaces, and our yards and gardens. We shape them with the furniture we put in them, the pictures we hang on the walls, the colors we choose. And they shape us. Find two or ten things you enjoy about your home and write about them.

.... My home is wonderful because ....

_____
_____
_____
_____
_____
_____
_____
_____
_____
_____
_____
_____
_____

What do I love about my neighborhood?

What is its special history, access, convenience to shopping, serenity, flowers, insects, birds, trees or other physical features? Why did you choose this place? What animals share your street?

.... *My neighborhood is great because* ....

_____
_____
_____
_____
_____
_____
_____
_____
_____
_____
_____
_____
_____
_____
_____
_____
_____
_____

What do I love about my
town or city?

What are its special features, peoples, events, climate, history, industry, and the like? What does your city have that no other on earth can claim?

..... My City ....

my bioregion

List special places, topography, landmarks, views, playgrounds, memories, energies, peoples, flora, fauna, and other highlights of your area.

....What I love about my bioregion....

_____
_____
_____
_____
_____
_____
_____
_____
_____
_____
_____
_____
_____
_____
_____
_____
_____
_____
_____
_____

What I love about my world .....

What are your special vacation spots, landmarks, plants, animals, countries, historical places, mountains, deserts, oceans, lakes, streams climates, and other earth treasures?

..... Is .....

_____
_____
_____
_____
_____
_____
_____
_____
_____
_____
_____
_____
_____
_____
_____
_____

Here is why my
historical time is special!

We live in an amazing historical moment. Only in the last two or three generations of Homo Sapiens' growth, an experience that spans over 7500 generations, have we had the incredible technologies we now take for granted every day. We live and breathe in an imaginal landscape of our own utopian dreams and our world would be literally unfathomable to our ancestors. Rudolph Steiner, the founder of Anthroposophy, said that we all are in love with our time. What do you love about this time in human and earth history?

.... Why do I love my time? ....

_____
_____
_____
_____
_____
_____
_____
_____
_____
_____
_____
_____

What can you say about your special place?

.... *Reflections on a special place* ....

Here is what I love about
this universe ....

Beauty, physics, rainbows, biology, chemistry, thunderstorms, diversity, science, mathematics, sunshine, complexity, infinity, particularity all can be experienced in our four dimensions of time and space. There may be non-physical realms in which the inhabitants cannot contemplate an ancient mountain or sit in a stable chair. There are tens, perhaps hundreds of millions of distinct species on our earth. To interact with something very strange is easy in our world but perhaps not so easy in others. To encounter difference, uniqueness, or novelty is easy here; just talk to your neighbor for verification. This is one of the definitions of an information rich environment – differences that make a difference. For what divine purpose was this domain created? What special features are contained in this realm that perhaps spiritual domains and other dimensions do not enjoy? What do you enjoy?

.... My Ode to Embodiment ....

_____
_____
_____
_____
_____
_____
_____
_____
_____

Describe your favorite place on Earth

.... Ode to Earth ....

What else can you say about your time, space and place? Is there a poem wanting to be written, a song sung, a dance to be choreographed? Is there a painting waiting to be born or some other art or craft to be awakened? Here is an open space and time to start.

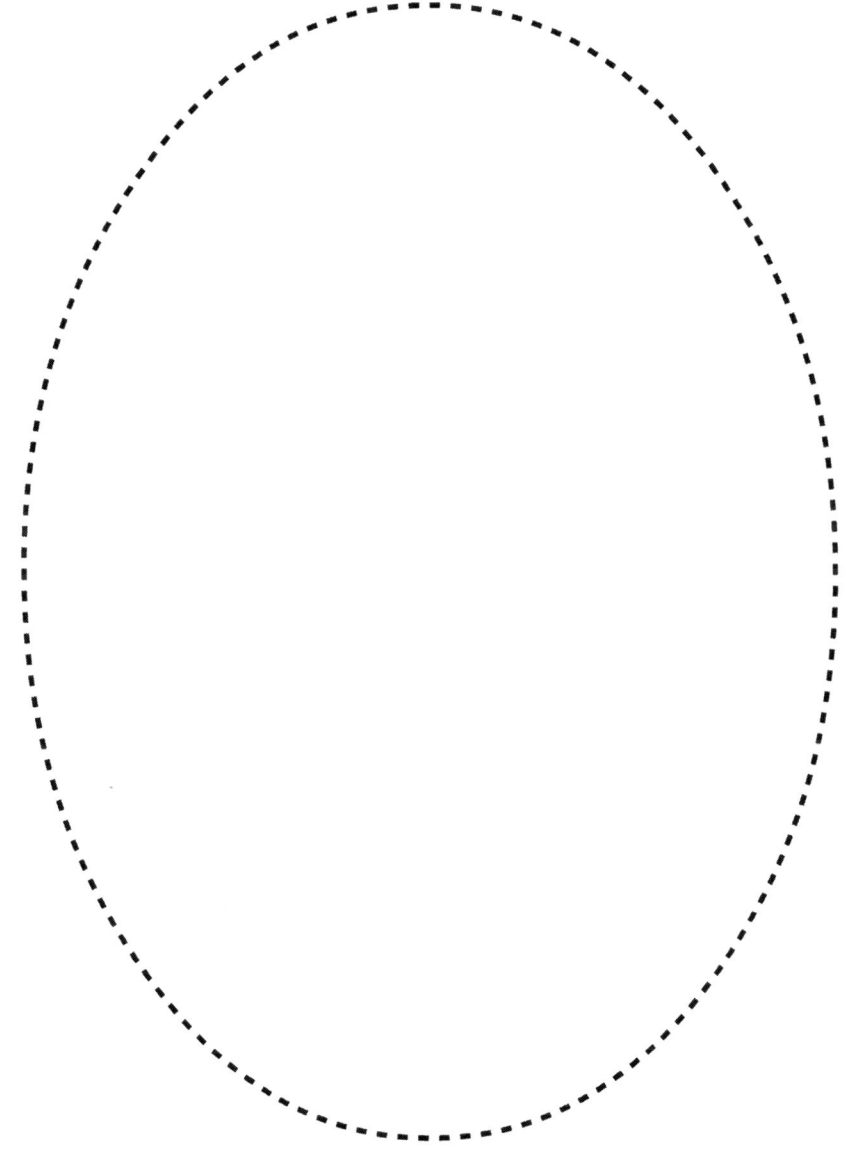

····Notes on Group Discussions····

Third Imaginal Exercise:
Loving Touch

Reach out and touch something or someone in a loving way!

Remember a time when you "touched" someone in a way that was positive for you and seemed to have positive effects for them. This touch could have been physical, psychological, musical, planned or spontaneous, such as an unexpected gift of some kind, anything that was an extension of yourself toward another with loving intent.

Then, remember a time when you were deeply touched by someone else.

Describe one experience in as much detail as you can, paying special attention to the feelings that arise in you body, heart, and mind. What images are invoked? What are the spiritual qualities that are co-incarnating through this exchange?

.... Can you describe your experiences? ....

.... *Reflections on Loving Touch* ....

Fourth Question

What do I love to do?

Play
Work
Hobbies
Relaxation
Inspiration
Learning
with others
by myself
to get energy moving

What I love to do at **Play?**

This is a big one. Play connects us with our joy and can lead deeper into a call to be more fully alive. For now, though, just imagine what it is that you enjoy doing on a regular basis. Do you like to play with your hands, you head, your heart? Is it watching TV? Toward which channels do you gravitate? Is it windsurfing, motorcycles, or board games you enjoy? Do you have fun with large groups or small, or by yourself? What are your favorite games, sports, and activities?

.... My Playground ....

_____
_____
_____
_____
_____
_____
_____
_____
_____
_____
_____
_____

I love to do
Work?

To find meaningful, enjoyable work is a singular blessing in a lifetime. And, if statistics are to be believed a large percentage of people actually enjoy their work - especially if it has purpose and connection to their values. What work do you love to do? Can you imagine your vocation and your avocations being the same activity?

....Here is the Work I love to do....

_____
_____
_____
_____
_____
_____
_____
_____
_____
_____
_____
_____
_____

Hobbies Anyone?

Do you have a Hobby? Is there something in the back of your mind you keep meaning to do but don't quite get around to it? Are you artistic, athletic, or musical? Can you cook? Do you like to do it? If you had the time for a hobby, what would it be?

.... My favorite Hobbies are ....

_____
_____
_____
_____
_____
_____
_____
_____
_____
_____
_____
_____
_____
_____
_____

Here is how I **Relax**

What do you do when you just are off the clock and relaxing? Can you revel in the sheer naked pleasure of kicking back and doing nothing productive?

.... *I relax by doing* ....

I am **Inspired** by

Everyone is capable of being inspired. We yearn for it in our stories, movies, celebrities, songs, politicians and leaders. Our homes can bring us comfort and safety but our visions brighten our lives, give us meaning and carry us through to the next horizon. I always get choked up when I hear Martin Luther King's, "I have a Dream" speech. What inspires you?

.... *Here are my Inspirations* ....

_____
_____
_____
_____
_____
_____
_____
_____
_____
_____
_____
_____
_____
_____
_____

I love to **Learn**

There are many different styles of learning. Some are quite academic while others are rooted in the body, motion, emotion, imagination or spirit. What processes seem to stimulate your growth and learning? What makes your sap flow?

....*I learn best by*....

_____
_____
_____
_____
_____
_____
_____
_____
_____
_____
_____
_____
_____
_____
_____
_____
_____

When I'm with **Others**

Name the conditions that you need to get into the flow with another person, with a small group, at a party with lots of people, in a large company situation, or other group conditions.

.... I collaborate best when ....

_____
_____
_____
_____
_____
_____
_____
_____
_____
_____
_____
_____
_____
_____
_____
_____

By Myself
I work **best** when

Some people work best with clean spaces. Others, like Albert Einstein, seem to prefer a rather cluttered space. Some like quiet, some like music, and some like the cacophony of the city. What conditions stimulate your flow?

.... *Personal flow space* ....

_____
_____
_____
_____
_____
_____
_____
_____
_____
_____
_____
_____
_____
_____
_____
_____
_____

Get **energy** moving!

All of us have times when we feel slow and low and out of the groove. What strategies do you use to pick yourself up? Do you exercise physically? Go to a music concert? Visit a museum? Go shopping? Do you seek solitude or crowds?

....*I tap energy by*....

..... Notes on Group Discussions .....

Fourth Imaginal Exercise
Go with the flow

All of us at one time or another have been "in the flow" or "in the groove". We found a sport in which we excelled, with a group of friends to which we belonged, or found ourselves on a college campus that fit us perfectly. Perhaps our creative work found us or we found ourselves in a profession, circle, or class for which we were made. We found our soul cluster or soul work or soul something. Maybe it was the people that helped stimulate our flow; being with close family, friends, or work colleagues.

Whatever circumstance you experienced or are experiencing one of the hallmarks of flow is an increased sense of participation and connection with life. There is a willingness to expend creative energy and a positive feedback from the environment. A wholeness emerges that is fostering to all concerned.

On the following page please list for yourself several times in which you were in the flow. Try to find situations for all of the preceding questions in this section,

What is being asked for here is a past experience that you can vividly recall in which you felt a strong sense of connection and participation with your activity, your world, with others and your life.

Then pick one of the times and describe it. What did it feel like; in your body, your mind and emotions, your heart and soul?

What are the qualities that you exhibit when you are expressing in the world in this manner?

.... Can you describe your experiences? ....

•••• *Reflections on Flow* ••••

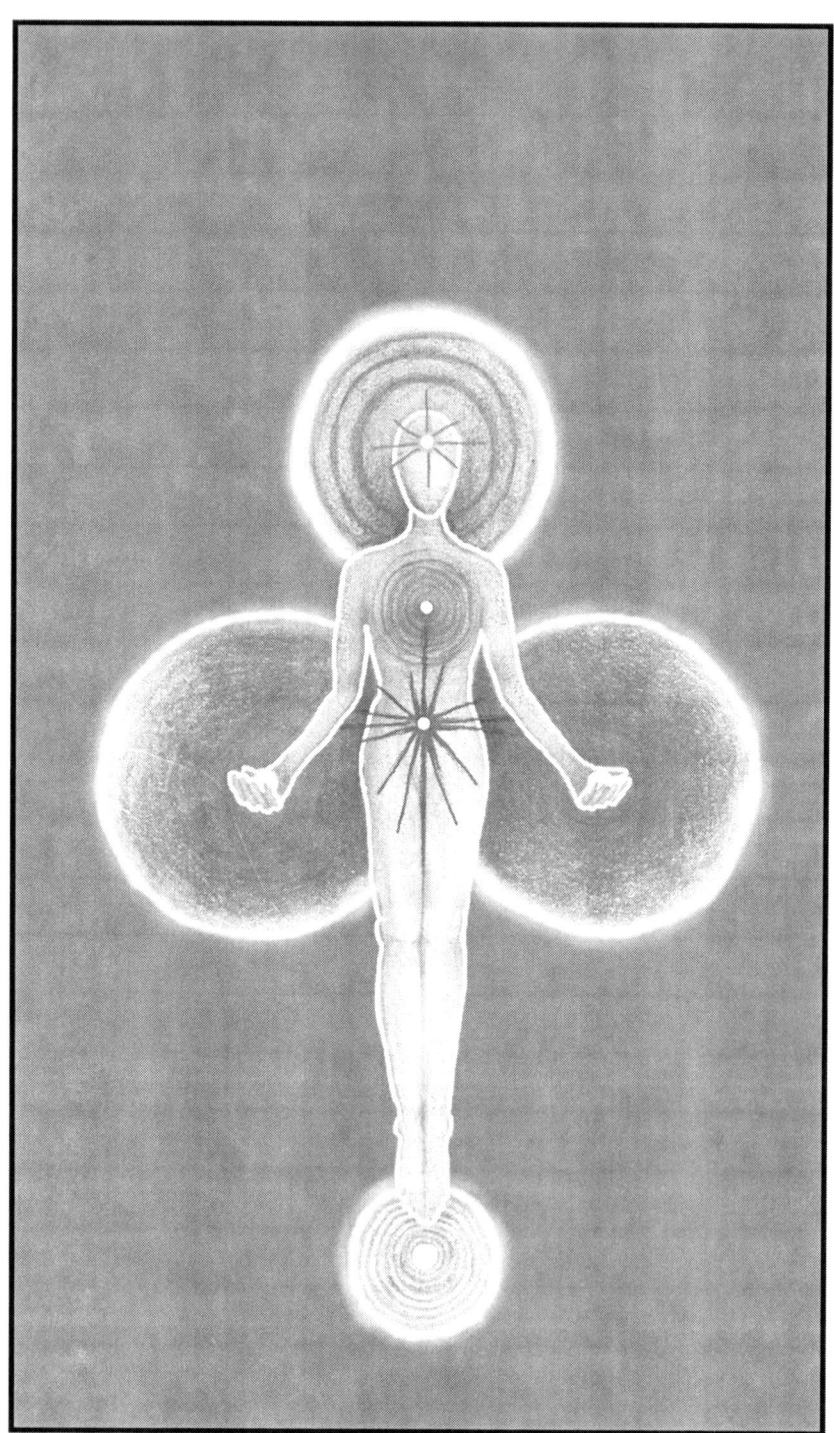

Section II: **Action**

I call this portion the "Inconvenient Journal" (with apologies to Al Gore) because it can be inconvenient to look at the actions we take in regards to loving ourselves, each other, the world, and our engagement with flow of life. Most of us engage in a lot of negative chatter to ourselves about these areas. I know I do!

This section can be seen as an opportunity to take fresh new steps and positive action which can release energy within us and around us in surprising ways.

First Question
What can I do to nurture myself?

Once again as in the previous section we suggest that you lay claim to what you appreciate about yourself. As a reminder and for convenience, here are the areas of loving self:

What do I love about myself?

my qualities

my talents

my ethics

my history

my ancestry

my body

my spirit

my _____?

In each area you discovered a special aspect of yourself. By acknowledging that which we love we invoke something in response. Our love does not go unrecognized. In fact it has the magical effect of waking something up within us and within our inner ecology.

This act of witnessing is a sacred healing force that we share. It is a source of strength and power to improve our relationship with each of these areas. What needs improvement? What needs healing? I can't say, but you can. So I invite you to go through the process once again and find one thing within each area that you would like to honor, clean up, pay more attention to, restore, or alchemize.

None of these actions need be extravagant or remarkable. What is important is that you consider these actions a gift to yourself and our world.

.... Here is how I will honor my qualities ....

....Here is how I will honor my talents....

....How I honor my personal history is....

.... This is how I honor my ancestry ....

.... Here is how I will honor my body....

.... *Here is how I will honor my spirit* ....

.... Here is how I will honor my _____? ....

....Notes on Group Discussions....

Notes on Group Discussions

Resources:
What can I do to nurture myself?

For a list of Lorian resources please refer to section V.

What follows is a list of slightly edited book and music references offered by the Lorian Community in response to my request for suggestions on what has been helpful to them in loving themselves. Some of their comments have also been included.

To start, here are music lyrics provided by Mike Scott of the *Waterboys* from the album *Bring 'Em All In*.

I'm learning to love him
to love and forgive
I'm learning to trust him
to let the man live
I'm learning to see him
to see who he is
I'm learning to love
the beauty he is

I'm learning to love him
to love and forgive
I'm learning to trust him
to let the man live
I'm learning to hold
his life in my hands
I'm learning to love
me just as I am

Adagio for Strings Music by Samuel Barber

A Psychology of Body, Soul. Spirit & Higher Knowing by Rudolph Steiner

Art is a Spiritual Path & Art is a Way of Knowing by Pat Allen

Body and Earth by Andrea Olsen

Care of the Soul & Dark Nights of the Soul by Thomas Moore

Creativity & Natural Grace by Matthew Fox

Field Notes on the Compassionate Life: a Search for the Soul of Kindness by Mac Ian Barasch

Finding Meaning in the Second Half of Life by James Hollis

If the Buddha Came to Dinner by Hale Sophia Schatz. This is a terrific book from a wonderfully wise woman. She is a remarkable woman, her focus is on nourishment and how we feed ourselves, physically and spiritually. Enjoy!

Juniper ,Wise Child & Colman by Monica Furlong (series for young people)

Learning to Love Yourself by Gay Hendricks

Letters to a Young Poet by Rainer Maria Rilke. He writes, "For one human being to love another; that is the most difficult of tasks, the ultimate, the last test of proof, the work for which all other work is but preparation."

Lost by David Waggoner

Memories, Dreams and Reflections by Carl Jung

Poetry of Hafiz

Poetry of Rumi

Sacred Contracts by Carolyn Myss

Simple Abundance by Sarah Ban Breathnach. One of the best authors and books I have ever had the pleasure of reading for loving oneself. The book reminds us that pleasure and joy is in everyday life if we simply notice our desires, and not be afraid to act upon them.

Soulcraft: Crossing into the Mysteries of Nature and Psyche by Bill Plotkin

Speigel im Speigel Music by Arvo Part

Start Where You Are: A Guide to Compassionate Living by Pema

Chodron. I love this book. It is really an amazing book on how to be more compassionate with ourselves and others.

Storycatcher: Making Sense of Our Lives through Power and Practice of Story by Christine Baldwin

The Dark Night of the Soul by Thomas Moore

The Five Things We Cannot Change by David Richo

The Physics of Angels by Matt Fox and Rupert Sheldrake

The Poetry of Self-Compassion CD by poet David Whyte, This CD is extraordinary. It was given to me by a friend at least 10 years ago and I have given many as a gift to friends who were struggling with some issue. One of the poems at the end of the lecture is called the Faces at Braga which is absolutely stunning in its capacity for self-love. I highly recommend the CD and his poetry to anyone.

The Second Half of Life by Angeles Arrien

The Wisdom of No Escape by Pema Chodron

Waking the Tiger by Peter Levine

Wild Geese by Mary Oliver (many people mentioned this author)

Women's Bodies, Women's Wisdom by Christianne Northrup

www.arthurzajonc.org/uploads/zajonc-love-and-knowledge.pdf (Editors note: this essay is highly recommended. It is written by an optical physicist - Arthur Zajonc- who clearly describes the necessity for being in the world with love.)

Second Question

What can I do to strengthen those I love?

Once again as in the previous section it is suggested that you lay claim to what you can do to strengthen others. As a reminder and for convenience, here are the earlier two questions:

Who do I love?
What are their special qualities?

By answering these questions you discovered special aspects of yourself and your love for others. By acknowledging that we love someone we invoke something in response. Our love does not go unrecognized. It can have the magical effect of waking something up within us and within the other person. This is a co-generated presence that we share. It is a source of strength and power to improve our relationship with each other. What needs improvement? What needs healing? Only you might know. So I invite you to go through the process once again and find one thing within each person that you would like to honor, clean up, restore, pay more attention to, or alchemize. None of these actions need be extravagant or remarkable. What is important is that you consider these actions a gift to yourself and to the ones you love.

Who do I love?

Please enter the people you listed in Section 1, Question 2. Then write next to their name a special thought, action, gift or remembrance that you bestow to them. The action can be trivial or large; the value is in the intent. Please note the special qualities you perceive in each person. How might you strengthen and nurture these qualities?

And, one of the greatest gifts we can give each other is space **without agenda.** It is common to wish specific outcomes for others or even try to impose a change that we feel might be in the other's best interest. But how often do we create a conscious free and open space for the other to hear the still small voice of spirit in their lives, a quiet space that allows them to recalibrate their internal compass and move in some unknown creative direction.

Name _____

Action, gift, or remembrance _____

_____

_____

_____

Would you like to give the gift of Open Space? _____

Name _____

Action, gift, or remembrance _____

_____

_____

Open Space? _____

Name _____

Action, gift, or **remembrance** _____

_____

_____

Open Space? _____

Name _____

Action, **gift,** or remembrance _____

_____

_____

Open Space? _____

Name _____

Action, gift, or remembrance _____

_____

_____

Open Space? _____

Name _____

Action, **gift**, or remembrance _____

_____

_____

Open Space? _____

Name _____

Action, gift, or remembrance _____

_____

_____

Open Space? _____

Notes on Group Discussions

Resources:
What can I do to strengthen those I love?

Once again, what follows is a slightly edited list of book, music and movie references offered by the Lorian Community in response to my request for their suggestions on what has been most helpful to them in loving others. Some of their comments have also been included.

Books and Music:

After the Ecstasy & The Laundry by Jack Kornfield
Dying Well by Ira Byock. A doctor with good stories to tell.
Everyday Blessings: the Inner Work of Mindful Parenting by Myla and Jon Kabat-Zinn. These parents put sovereignty at the center of their family relationships.
Experiences With The Dying And The Dead by Claire Blatchford
Fidelity: Five Stories, Watch With Me: and Six Other Stories of the Yet & *The Memory of Old Jack* by Wendell Berry
Gilead by Marilynne Robinson. A small town preacher's remembrances of his life lived. It deals with the theme of blessings and much more. It is very thoughtful and quiet reading. I was blessed by this.
Hymn to the Russian Earth Music from the album, *Concert for the Earth* by the Paul Winter Consort
Kinship With All Life by J. Allen Boone. Stories of communicating with animals with respect.
Kitchen Table Wisdom by Rachel Naomi Remen. These are amazing stories and I've learned so much from her. She's a real listener, a doctor, and a gentle and true story teller.
Love Poems From God Translated by Daniel Ladinsky. They're a collection of verses from the East and the West; all the way from Rabia, to Rumi, to Hafiz to St. John of the Cross. They're deep,

funny, startling, very much on the mark.

Loving What Is by Byron Katie

Loving Who shows Up by Eric Dowsett

Miracle of Love: Stories about Neem Karoli Baba by Ram Dass. Neem Karoli Baba was Ram Dass' guru.

Nonviolent Communication: A Language of Life by Marshall Rosenberg. We love by the way we communicate.

Raising an Emotionally Intelligent Child: The Heart of Parenting by John Gottman with Forward by Daniel Goleman. He models a style of parenting that honors sovereignty non-violently, as well as mentors a child as he gets in touch with feelings, needs, emotions or "what is going on" and coaches him through to creative problem solving.

Strange News From Another Star from the book, "Augustus" by Hermann Hesse. A great and moving story about learning to love others.

The Chosen by Chaim Potok. The movie or book is recommended and is about the loving friendship between a liberal and an orthodox Jewish boy.

The Coming of the Cosmic Christ and Original Blessing by Matthew Fox

The Country of Marriage by Wendell Berry (poems) and anything else written by Mr. Berry.

The Politics of Meaning: Restoring Hope and Possibility in an Age of Cynicism by Michael Lerner. He is president and co-founder of Commonweal and the Smith Farm Center for the Healing Arts in Washington, DC.

Movies:

A Windy Day This is a short animated film by John and Faith Hubley using the taped conversation of their young daughters.

Life Is Beautiful Vita è bella (Italian 1997) Movie is about a Jewish man, who falls in love with a non-Jewish lady

Love Actually This was a holiday film several years ago that features an ensemble cast. As its name suggests, the film is largely about love, and it portrays a number of different, and in some cases unusual, forms of loving others.

Monster's Ball I saw this one several years ago, and the following summary is a bit of a "spoiler" also. Halle Berry won an Academy Award for her portrayal of an African-American woman who becomes involved in a relationship with a man (Billy Bob Thorton) from a racist family. In this film, as I remember it, there's a lot of juxtaposition of love and hatred.

Ponette 1996 French film directed by Jacques Doillon

Pursuit of Happiness Will Smith (playing Chris Gardner, if I remember correctly, and based on a true story) demonstrates great love for and dedication to his young son.

The Green Mile This is a film about an empath whose love takes the form of voluntarily taking on the negative energies that are causing suffering in others, which he often does in the service of healing.

The Hobart Shakespeareans This was a PBS special that I think reflects the love of a teacher for his middle school students.

Third Question

What can I do to nurture the places I love?

In the previous section we suggested that you claim the physical places that are meaningful to you. As a reminder and for convenience here are the domains in which you worked.

home
neighborhood
town or city
bioregion
world
historical time
special space or place
&
my overall physical universe

In each realm you discovered your organic connections to your living ecology.

I invite you to go through the process again and find one thing within each area that you would like to honor, clean up, restore, pay more attention to, or alchemize. *None of these actions need be extravagant or remarkable.*

What is important is that you acknowledge your connection to and engagement with your place. Consider these actions a gift to a friend or family member or lover.

....Here is my gift to my home....

....Here is my gift to my neighborhood....

.... Here is my gift to my Town or City ....

_____
_____
_____
_____
_____
_____
_____
_____
_____

.... Here is my gift to my Bioregion ....

_____
_____
_____
_____
_____
_____
_____
_____
_____

.... *Here is my gift to my World* ....

.... *Here is my gift to my time* ....

....Here is my gift to my special space....

....My gift to my physical universe is....

....Notes on Group Discussions....

.... *Notes on Group Discussions* ....

Resources:
What can I do to nurture the places I love?

Once again, what follows is a slightly edited list of book, music and movie references offered by the Lorian Community in response to my request for suggestions on what has been most helpful to them in loving the world. Some of their comments have also been included.

Books and Music:

A Place on Earth by Wendell Berry, (novel) *Remembering* (novel) *The Gift of Good Land* (essays)

American Primitive by Mary Oliver, (Pulitzer Prize for Poetry) and anything else by Mary Oliver (awareness of natural forces / plants & animals /elements /life)

Blessing: The Art and the Practice & The Call by David Spangler

Emergence of Ecofeminism by Irene Diamon & Gloria Femon Ornstein

Farming: A Handbook (poetry) and anything else by Wendell Berry (rural American farming, stewardship of land & culture, generations of caring men & women on the land)

Hand to Earth by Andy Goldsworthy

Last Child in the Woods: Saving Our Children from Nature Deficit Disorder by Richard Louv

Local and regional Field Guides, Of anything ! and everything ! Native plants, trees, shrubs, birds, bugs, mammals, amphibians, fishes, geology, mosses, lichens, mushrooms, liverworts... get to know your neighbors !!

Music by Paul Winter

Music by the Turtle Island String Quartet

Mutual Causality in Buddhism and General Systems Theory by Joanna Macy

My Story as Told by Water by David James Duncan. Essays on NW the health of watersheds, rivers, creeks.

Nature tracking books by Tom Brown

Pilgrim at Tinker Creek by Annie Dillard

Reflections Yale Divinity School's journal

Sacred Earth (autumn edition 2007) Parabola magazine

Songs for Coming Home, Where Many Rivers Meet, Fire in the Earth and *The House of Belonging* by David Whyte

Sun Dancing by Geoffrey Morehouse

The Earth's Imagination & Powers of the Universe by Brian Swimme

The Education of Little Tree by Forrest Carter (novel: a Cherokee boyhood in the 1930's) A very special book, read this aloud to your kids and grandkids.

The Great Work & The Dream of the Earth by Thomas Berry

The Man Who Killed the Deer, People of the Valley, The Woman of Otawi Crossing by Frank Waters (all novels) and anything else by Frank Waters. He explores layers of human culture in place in the Southwest and spent years living and studying with the Hopi.

The Man Who Planted Trees by Jean Giono. This is a short, sweet, inspiring awe, also a very good read aloud.

The Meadow by James Galvin. A mixture of novel and natural history.

The Road Not Taken: A Selection of Poems by Robert Frost,

The Spell of the Sensuous by David Abram. A little more difficult to read: shifting our perception of human perception of nature /animate relationships /active relationship with earthy elements.

The Way of Ignorance : And Other Essays by Wendell Berry

To Honor the Earth, Seeds of Inspiration & To Hear the Angels Sing by Dorothy Maclean

Turtle Island by Gary Snyder (another Pulitzer for poetry - beat poet, zen buddha-dharma practice, backcountry lookout, 70's homesteader, ecology /wilderness spokesperson) Also, *The Practice of the Wild: Essays, Riprap and Cold Mountain Poems, Mountains and Rivers without End, Left out in the Rain & No Nature* and anything else by Gary Snyder

Where Many Rivers Meet by David Whyte. Along with several books of poems, David Whyte has also published two wonderful non-fiction books on work as love; *Crossing the Unknown Sea: Work As a Pilgrimage of Identity and The Heart Aroused: Poetry and the Preservation of the Soul in Corporate America*

Winter Gardening in the Maritime Northwest by Binda Colebrook. This has been a favorite for loving the Puget Sound actively through gardening in her enviable growing climate.

Wonderful Life by Stephen Jay Gould

Baraka in Judaism, a blessing usually recited during a ceremony

Movies:

Into Great Silence (Die Große Stille) is a documentary film directed by Philip Gröning that was first released in 2005

Microcosmos: Le Peuple de L'Herbe (Microcosmos: The grass people) is a documentary film by Claude Nuridsany and Marie Pérennou produced by Jacques Perrin. This film is primarily a record of detailed insect interactions set to the music of Bruno Coulais.

Spring, Summer, Fall, Winter…and Spring The seasons in the title mark the passage of time and symbolize the stages in the life of man.

The Earth's Imagination This is a video series hosted by Brian Swimme Center for the Study of the Universe.

Fourth Question

How can I nurture the natural *flow* of what I love to do?

When we are doing what we love we naturally step into the flow of life. It is a gift to be home in our own skin and to appreciate how we connect with our own ways of doing things. So how can we nourish ourselves in ways that keep our energy moving and link us with the deep flow of life?

What does it mean to be in the world with soul, with spirit, with flow? This question of course has many answers but an interesting experience altered my view of this.

One day a group of people associated with Lorian were having a discussion at a friend's home. I forget what the topic was but as we were talking, I became aware of a presence surrounding one of the people in the group and then others. Perhaps it was the part of the person's soul which engages the earth through incarnation.

Whatever it was this fluid life presence was continually attempting to express itself in a natural, organic, and comfortable way. It was wholly at home in this world, a quiet artesian well bubbling forth to express itself and splash into the community of life. And it was constantly being high-jacked by anxiety, fear of making the wrong impression, prior set agendas, important purposes, lack of self worth, and a host of other energetic ruts with which we irrigate our hurts.

Later this got me thinking about how I block my natural soul's flow into the world. What do I do to high-jack my gifts of presence, love, life and joy to myself and this world? Well, for one, I can hold a hurt of a perceived wrong. So I am learning how to forgive. I also can be a bulldozer and overly sure of myself and ……….. well, you get the picture.

What do you do to high-jack yourself? Where are the blocks that leave you enervated? What can you do about them?

Once again here is the previous list and question.

What do I love to do?

Play
Work
Hobbies
Relaxation
Inspiration
Learning
with others
by myself
to get energy moving

The following pages ask how we high-jack ourselves and how we can improve the situation. Please feel free to add your own. Consider these a gift to yourself to release bound up energy for creative work and play.

.... How do I block playful energy? ....

_____
_____
_____
_____
_____
_____
_____
_____
_____
_____

.... Here is my corrective plan ....

_____
_____
_____
_____
_____
_____
_____
_____
_____
_____

.... *How do I block productive energy?* ....

.... *Here are ways to love my work*....

.... *How do I block my creative energy?* ....

.... *Will a hobby help?* ....

.... *How do I really relax?* ....

.... *Plans for relaxation* ....

.... How do I find inspiration? ....

.... Plans for Inspiration ....

.... *Have I become closed to new ideas?* ....

.... *Ways to nurture my learning* ....

....Am I comfortable with people?....

....How might I be more comfortable?....

....Am I comfortable with myself?....

....Time for Solitude?....

.... *What primarily blocks my energy?* ....

.... *Resources to release the dam?* ....

Notes on Group Discussions

Resources:
How can I nurture the natural flow of what I love to do?

Once again, what follows is a slightly edited list of book references offered by the Lorian Community in response to my request for suggestions on what has been most helpful to them in connecting to the underlying sacred flow of life. Some of their comments have also been included.

Books:

Awakening Through Love: Unveiling Your Deepest Goodness by John Makransky

God, I Am by Peter O. Erbe. The book that, to me, fits all four categories of teaching loving. It has been an endless source of inspiration to me over the many times I have read it.

Rilke's Book of Hours: Love Poems to God by Anita Barrows & Joanna Macy, (the translated poetry of Rainier Maria von Rilke)

The Call by David Spangler. This should be required reading for anyone who has ever wished to find their soul's purpose and spiritual call.

The Essential Rumi, Coleman Barks

The Gift: Poems by Hafiz, Daniel Ladinsky, (the translated poems of the Sufi mystic)

The Last of the Just by Andre-Schwarz-Bart. This book is about the endless love of the Jewish people for God and from God to his Jewish people, although paradoxically it goes into the Holocaust.

The Practice of the Presence of God Brother Lawrence

The Song of Songs (of Solomon) in the Old Testament

Under the Tuscan Sun (film only—book very different, not as good, though it's usually the other way around!)

More Recommendations:

Websites: http://

brughjoy.com Brugh Joy
catherinemaccoun.com Catherine Macoun
cofc.edu/~rels/irwin3.htm Lee Irwin
dreampower.com R.J. Stewart
earthcharter.org
findhorn.org
gatekeeper.org.uk
genesisfarm.org
gratefulness.org
hallowquest.org.uk John Matthews
hallowquest.org.uk Caitlin Matthews
heavenletters.org
herondance.org
joanborysenko.com Joan Borysenko
mossdreams.com Robert Moss
pachamama.org
qigongseattle.org
springspreserve.org
thearchdruidreport.blogspot.com John Michael Greer
whidbeyinstitute.org
wild.org
williambloom.com William Bloom
zoence.co.uk
www.arthurzajonc.org

Section III: Psychic Recycling

Becoming a Planetary Superfun Site

We are always generating a lot of stuff into our environment. We are also receiving a lot. This is not a radical statement and applies to much more than our physical consumption, waste streams and physical pollution.

We all have had the experience of saying or doing something nice or nasty and seeing the effects of our action. Too, we have all been the recipient of another's actions. The fields of law and ethics rest on the assumption that we are capable of choice and therefore worthy of blame or praise, rewards or punishments. What is choice if it is not the capacity to generate one type of action over another?

But now we are taking this a bit further. The suggestion here is that not only can we affect our world (which, by the way, includes our interior worlds) by physical action related to the five senses, but we can also do so through our energy, emotions, minds, spirit and overall presence.

Again this is not an overly radical idea. We all have had the experience of having a grumpy friend bring us down or jubilant children lift our spirits. Ideas generated by scientists, philosophers, religious teachers and the like have had huge effects on civilization. Imagine the twentieth century without the phenomenal idea that energy and matter are interchangeable; Einstein's $E=MC^2$. No Hiroshima, no nuclear arms race, in short, a much different world.

But how about a critical thought or kind statement? These too have effects. We entrain to one another quite naturally. I remember seeing a wonderful TV program that documented how we tend to adapt the posture of one another as we converse. Our life energy, sometime called our "chi", can affect the world too. The emerging and ancient fields of energy healing and energy work attest to our ability to act upon each other energetically.

Speaking spiritually, we have many examples in literature of teachers, adepts, gurus, masters, saints and the like who have a profound effect on others. Remember Jesus asking who touched the hem of his garment when he felt the power flow out of him? Ammachi travels the world giving "Darsham" hugs to people. Many report amazing inner and outer experiences. Many more examples could be given and it is probably safe to say that you, the reader, have had such experiences. Maybe it was a friend or lover, a teacher or co-worker, a child's birth or an encounter with an animal, a grove of trees or a flower. Whatever it was conferred something ineffable, something wonderful, something that changed the way you see the world. This experience is quite common, if we are to believe the surveys of such things.

Anyway, the point is that we are living in an interwoven world that has real effects on our physical bodies, our energy levels, our emotions, our thoughts, and our spiritual lives. We are not an island! Or are we?

Well, in a way, we are an island since we are not totally conditioned by all of these effects. We can act not just react! Parenthetically, Dorothy Maclean, one of the three founders of the Findhorn Foundation considers this statement one of the cornerstones of a spiritual education. Why is this is an important concept? If we are capable of evaluating the flow of energy and information coming to us and deciding what to do with it, that is to keep it, reject it or transform it, we have established that we are not just a cog in the machinery of life. We are an alchemical vessel! And like islands we are formed in the volcanic fire of the cosmos flowing forth from deep in the galactic ocean, fundamentally connected and kin to all life.

So what does this all have to do with energy hygiene? During the course of a day or a lifetime or many lifetimes, if you are inclined to think that way, we can pick up a lot of toxicity. We also can pick up a lot of nutrition but it is not always easy to tell the difference. For example; I am in the market for a new car. I'm not sure what would fit the bill for the next stage of my life because I am not sure of all the activity the next stage might require. Then I see a car advertisement (or thirty) which excites me. Does it mean that this is the car for me? Or is it just the compact energy, a sweet packet of designed will from the advertising energy high jacking and manipulating my perceived need? How would I tell?

I could spend a great deal of time analyzing myself, my needs and my finances and perhaps arrive at a satisfactory answer. Perhaps I could consult a friend or spouse to help me decide. I could also ask the salesman what he thought.

Ultimately, whatever is decided, it should be consistent with the deepest flow of my life; my "call" to be part of this earth and participate in this domain. Not all decisions might have powerful effects on this call but some will and it is not always easy to tell which ones. The safest route is to find a way to stand in the flame of my being and check. That is step number two but first let's shake off a little dust and grime.

A Personal Story

It has been my good fortune to participate in and witness various Native American Lakota ceremonies. The sweat lodge is something with which I am most familiar although by no means am I anything other than an onlooker to this rich tradition. A good friend of mine, Bruce Govan, is a well known singer and drummer and he sometimes lets me tag along.

Anyway, he invited me along one Sunday afternoon and as I respected the man pouring the lodge and Bruce who was singing, I gladly accepted. As usual we spent some time creating prayer ties, smudging, covering the poles of the lodge with blankets and black plastic (Buffalo hides are in short supply) and generally preparing ourselves in an inner way to enter the lodge. Having done this several times before, I was anticipating a good cleansing sweat and prayerful gathering.

When the time came, stripped to our shorts, we each in turn circled the large fire which was heating the stones, turned to the four directions and saying "Mitaku Oyasin" (Lakota for "all my relations") we crawled into the lodge. The first set of stones were reverently brought forth, laid in the center pit, and arranged with a deer antler. The door flap was closed and the first of four rounds began in the red hot glow of the stones.

As anyone who has participated in a sweat lodge knows it can get pretty intense with steam when the water is poured over the glowing stones. The swirling moist heat quickly overwhelms the small enclosed space. Generally, though, it is not intended to create an endurance test but rather a focus for prayer, spiritual cleansing and insight. This had been my previous experience.

This time, however, as the prayers began, I began to get violently ill. My whole body seemed to be rebelling at the experience. I tried to call out to open the door and let me escape but found no voice strong enough to be heard. I moaned prostrate on the dirt floor of the lodge in agony. Fortunately, after an excruciatingly long time, the one officiating the lodge, the pourer, was sensitive enough to know something amiss. He opened the door and had everyone file out – something I have never before or since experienced.

Gratefully I crawled out and squatted on a wooden stump trying to collect myself. As I did so a beautiful feeling and vision came. I could see many of the foibles of humanity, mine and the others of our assembled company, floating like small cinders on a sea of **golden liquid light**. The stuff we had accumulated throughout our lives were burned and purified as they touched this warm lava like substance, like dross on molten iron.

I felt instantly well and a few minute later, when the next round was started I happily went back into the lodge and enjoyed the next three rounds.

Later, telling Bruce of this experience, he said that this lodge had been created to help heroin, cocaine, alcohol and drug addicts find a way to purify themselves. That was the group with whom we were sharing the lodge. I had picked up the stuff they were discarding! Laughingly, he told me that he always made a number of protection prayer ties when he entered this kind of ceremony. I thanked him for his belated help by suggesting he might try walking barefoot on hot asphalt.

Why tell this story? Three reasons. One, it shows that we can pick up harmful stuff from our environment that is not really ours. Two, it shows that we have resources within us to deal with this toxicity. These resources can arise spontaneously as in my story or we can work at it as in the following exercise. And three it shows the possibility of shielding ourselves against unhealthy influences.

The first part of the exercise that follows is designed to help us safely slough off those elements that have superficially attached themselves to us and are harmful to us and not part of our overall life and work. They are like viruses which can redirect our life energies away from healthy tasks and into reproducing themselves. It is a good thing to be rid of them but they are not evil in and of themselves. They are simply out of ecological place.

The second part of the exercise is designed to help us align with our own resources of life and regeneration; the part of us that knows our deep identity (our psychic immune system if you will) and knows what to keep and what to discard.

The third part is intended to help build up our natural psychic immune system. One capable of discerning what is good for us as we encounter the worlds around and within us.

One last thought. In the exercise you will note a step that suggests calling forth a helper to collect the garbage so to speak. This idea is not always included as part of exercises of these types so a word of explanation is in order.

In times past our ancestors living with much less population density could safely discard their waste into the stream of life quite casually. They lived in such a way and in such numbers that they did not tax the ability of the eco-system to purify the waste - which was anyway rather low grade and organic.

However, as man has grown in numbers and in creative sophistication in regards to chemical and atomic constructions we can no longer safely discard our waste. We still do it, much more than we should, but nearly everyone recognizes that it is a bad idea. There is an exact analog to **psychic waste**.

Ideally we would not see ourselves as generating waste but rather directing resources into the proper place to become once again part of the free flow of life. We would want to recycle the waste with a proper disposal company capable of handling the material, whatever it is. The same holds true for our energetic recycling. We can no longer simply throw the stuff aside, like bones of a mastodon, and let the earth take care of it.

So, we ask for someone or something – some being of sufficient configuration – to come forth and scoop up the material to be recycled.

There is no need to get elaborate about it. We can simply ask for help to come forward and know that our request, imagination, and intent are enough to attract the action that is needed, like crows to road kill. For me this is a bunch of little rowdy rock guys who can absorb energy and dive back into the molten core of the earth. For you it could be whatever strikes your fancy; an angel, a nature force, whatever. If nothing comes to mind just know that the help is there to collect the recycling – like the truck that comes to your house. Let them go to do their job. It is not your work to follow them or worry after them, just to call them. Heck, they are happy to comply; few people bother to ask!

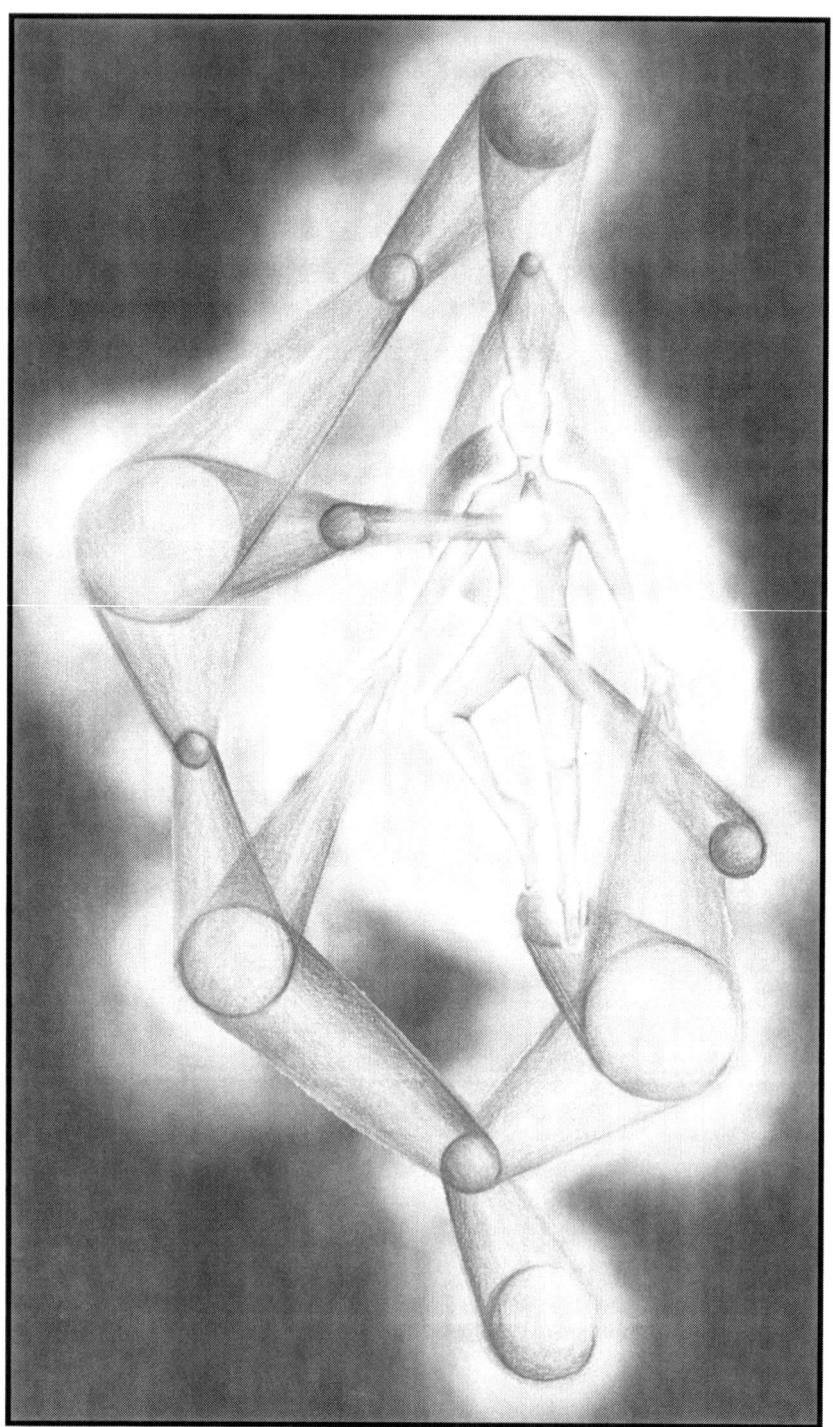

Exercise: Protection and Cleansing

Part One

If you can, start by taking a walk or doing some type of aerobic exercise outside. Breathe deep and let the natural world and its inner life caress and nurture your being. Get in the sunshine if possible and enjoy the fact that you are a living organism supported by the miracle of photosynthesis; the amazing process of photons being transmuted into sugar, of light becoming organic substance, of the word becoming flesh. This is our heritage; the ability to transform light into life. Enjoy yourself. The best energy hygiene – one that even opens the gates beyond death – is a good laugh and joyful dance.

You can now return home to a comfortable favorite chair or continue your walk. Next imagine a being, place, process, or container that could handle any negative substance that you might discard.

Once you have the sense that recycling help is near shake off the stuff on your surface, like a big puppy shaking off the water from a dive in the pond. There is no need to identify any of the stuff, just imagine that whatever it is no longer is attached to you. If a particular image or feeling passes through you at this stage be thankful and let it go!

Part Two

Now let us go a little deeper. Relax, know that you are supported in this work by protective forces and beings, by your own cleansing, by those you love and love you, and by the nature of this activity. When you feel ready, create in your imagination a doorway. If you are home imagine that this is a new door, one that you have just discovered. If you are outside see your self stepping through a portal into a new landscape. Through this door/portal is a wonderful scene of nature with a golden river flowing through it. However this appears to you, go with the flow.

Step into the scene, be part of the landscape. It is safe and protected by your attunement to those beings who align with such power. The golden river flows from a place you cannot quite see, perhaps high in the mountains of this magical land or from some deep eternal fountainhead. It is the river of your god-self. It flows out beyond your sight subducted into the molten core of the earth and beyond. In between is a golden pool of gently swirling liquid light. The sky is white-bright blue, the birds are chirping and the temperature of a slight breeze is just perfect. All is right with the world. You are drawn to the pool, find it warm and responsive to the touch like a living force. You wade in and lower yourself deep into the healing balm. You feel more and more buoyant while you sink and note that old feelings, hurts and memories are flowing out of you. These become white foam and are carried downstream by the flow. They are the residue of that which is no longer yours to carry. You feel at peace and know that you are being cleansed. After a time you emerge feeling vibrant, alive, fresh, bathed in radiance, and ready to take on the world!

Part Three

Step back through the door into the everyday world. If you like, see this golden stream expanding out around your body like a warm glow. Let it assist you at the boundary when you encounter the world. Let that glow fill your senses. Feel the goodness in your whole body from tip to toes. Touch the world around you with soft eyes, let this feeling flow into the earth through your feet and into the air on your breath. Touch something lovingly with your hands and let it touch you back. You are Eve, you are Adam, awake to the first day of creation.

Ending

Return to your everyday state knowing that you can travel back to the golden river of liquid light anytime you wish. Do something everyday and ordinary like raid the refrigerator!

Further Resources:

This exercise has many variations. Please feel free to adapt it to yourself in whatever way you like. In addition there are many more magical, ceremonial, mystical, shamanic, psychological and other ways of working to achieve the same effects. For a more detailed and complete look at spiritual hygiene three books are recommended:

Feeling Safe or *Psychic Protection* by William Bloom, and *Psychic Shield: The Personal Handbook of Psychic Protection* by Caitlin Matthews.

Section IV: **Embodying Eden**

Embodying Eden
Exercise:

This is the core exercise of this book and the one to which all the others have been building. The basic idea for this exercise was developed by David Spangler. I first encountered it as the foundation for a world blessing ritual in one of his weekend workshops called Embodying the World. Over the years I have modified and used it in many ways and in various forms as has he.

As a spiritual exercise it is unusual in that it is not trying to lead away from this world into a transcendental state but rather into a state of increased connection and engagement with this world. It is from this interactive space that new possibilities emerge for experiencing our natural wholeness and partnering with the organic intelligences of this domain and the deep ecologies of other worlds. The personal platform it forms can build a safe foundation for working in co-creative partnership with many domains of earth and spirit.

It is intrinsically simple and can be done while sitting, standing, or walking. It can be physically enacted by facing one of the four directions and turning to the right through the progressions of each stage. Or, it might be done imaginally while walking outside. There are seven directions which are active in this exercise. The direction of:

1. Spirit - Above
2. Earth - Below
3. Oneself - Front
4. Humanity - Right
5. Gaia - Back
6. Flow - Left
7. Sacredness – Inward Wholeness

Preparation

First do some kind of cleansing or purification activity. One example is the exercise offered in this book. This is done mostly for getting in the mood and shifting consciousness away from everyday concerns and toward a deeper wholeness that is our natural birthright. Think of it as getting ready for a special event.

Steps:

One:
Once you have established your clear space and intent begin by asking for protection from any spiritual forces with which you might feel connected.

Two:
Ask that you be nurtured by our living planet with which you have chosen to share life.

Three:
Recall the exercises you did around loving yourself. Feel back into the sensations of loving yourself. Imagine now that you are a generative creative power standing as a radiant source of light for the world, a living gift and blessing.

Four:
Recall the exercises you did around loving others. What were your felt senses surrounding the people whom you love? Imagine their love radiating back to you. Together you are forming a beautiful bright glow of warmth and lovingness. You are the love of Humanity. You are Humanity expressing its true intent to offer itself to this world.

Five:
Recall the exercises you did around the places that you love. How do you feel when you bask in the glory of your favorite spot on this magnificent Earth? Imagine a liquid light arising from the earth and surrounding you, bathing you in the lush organic life of the planet. Together you form a gathering green radiance that offers its torch like a beacon in the loving embrace of a bright spiral galaxy.

Six:
Recall now the flow you found within yourself. What do you feel when you are in tune and moving in harmony with life? Imagine the great flow of cosmic life; the sap in the trees, the crashing waves of the ocean, blood coursing through infinite arteries, the quiet growth of ancient trees, the noiseless swirl of the earth in frictionless space, the birth of stars, the blaze of the solar winds. Feel into the rhythms of life in all its wonder.

Seven:
In all of this you stand. You are part of the grand symphony of life. Now imagine each light beginning to flow into the center where you stand; the flame of Self, the glow of Humanity, the green iridescence of this world, the shining river of life itself. Feel the protection and participation of your spiritual allies and earth energies holding and supporting and radiating around and within with you. Let the sacred be born anew in your midst. Feel Eden embodied afresh in you.

Closing:
Offer a blessing to the world, to whomever you wish, to yourself and to the great mystery of life. Touch something in your surrounding with love and nurturing. Feel its response.

When you feel complete, give thanks to all those who aided in your work and to yourself for offering a gift to the world. Then move about and do something everyday to shift the energy back to your everyday world. Raid the refrigerator, do some exercises and connect back with everyday reality.

Exercise: Variation

You can also do this exercise imagining yourself once again as a tree.

1. Your leaves transfigure sunlight and the stars
2. Your roots drink deep of the nurturing earth
3. You stand whole in the trunk and branches of your identity
4. You participate in the life of the primal forest
5. You are engaged with the green life of the world
6. Sap flows up and down your trunk and limbs, you breathe life
7. You bring fresh possibilities and blessings to the creatures who share your space. A new Eden is born.

Section V: Where to from here?

The Lorian Association offers a variety of mechanisms to support the practices suggested by this workbook.

There are four modules in the basic Starshaman Training program* which can be purchased as home study materials:

- Home-Crafting: Self, Sacred and Blessing
- Space-Crafting: The Incarnational Self
- Crafting Inner Alliances: Working with Spiritual Forces
- World-Crafting: Manifestation and Service

Please contact Lorian Press for availability.

Starshaman Training Online

All four Starshaman Home Mystery School™ Training Modules are also available as three-month long online classes.

Starshaman Training Weekend Intensives

We also offer a three-day face-to-face weekend intensive with each of the Starshaman Online classes. These workshops give an abbreviated form of the material contained in the corresponding module.

Walking Whole:
Incarnational Spiritual Practice

The Walking Whole program is a series of short one-day and two-day workshops offering training in specific skills that embody the principles of Incarnational Spirituality (IS). Each can be taken separately. The emphasis is on practice and the practical use of the IS concepts in one's daily life, presented in short, accessible formats.

Mailing List, David's Desk, Newsletters

If you are on our mailing list, you will receive every two weeks an article from David Spangler called "David's Desk," a monthly e-newsletter, and announcements about special activities and classes.

The Lorian Associates

The Lorian Associates make up our growing community of people engaged with applying Incarnational Spirituality in their lives and sharing the results with each other. The only requirement for participation is to a working knowledge of Incarnational Spirituality. We are currently working to develop a social networking site to support the Associates with online community capabilities for mutual sharing and communication. Please check our website to see when this may become available.

Workshops, Talks, Online Classes & Forums

Occasionally, Lorian sponsors online classes, face to face talks, workshops and forums around specific themes or books. These vary in length from a few hours to several weeks. Sometimes

David Spangler hosts a forum in which he is simply available for questions and discussion. Check with the website for availability.

Advanced Programs and Training

Lorian also offers advanced training and longer-term programs for those who both wish them and qualify. Such programs can lead to a Masters Degree in Contemporary Spirituality. Be sure to check with us about what is available.

Soul Friending

We can recommend several trained Spiritual Directors/Soul Friends associated with Lorian. They work with clients in person and by phone to deepen into their experience of the sacred, develop their spiritual practice, and work through personal spiritual blocks and opportunities.

Check the Website www.lorian.org

Our website regularly has articles to read, updates and announcements about classes—including new, special classes that may not fit in one of our regular programs—and other goodies. Check by regularly to see what's new and what's available.

Thank you!

About the Author

Jeremy Berg is owner of the Lorian Press and past director of the Lorian Association. He is a workshop presenter and well publicized architectural designer specializing in energy efficiency. He holds a certificate in Spiritual Direction, has taught at both the secondary and post secondary level and has been a dean and college vice president. Various forms and practices of spirituality, especially an applied incarnational approach, has been a passion for many years.

Printed in the United States
107767LV00002B/415-423/P